CHRISTUS
VICTOR

CHRISTUS VICTOR

In His Quest to Destroy Evil and Restore All Things Ruined by Evil

BOYD W. MORRIS

BASILEIA
PUBLISHING

Basileia Publishing
P.O. Box 60695
Colorado Springs, CO 80960

Basileia Publishing is the publishing arm of Basileia, a future-oriented, Celtic-inspired, missional expression of the Church in ecclesiastical fellowship with *Communio Christiana*. Basileia (which means "kingdom") imagines, cultivates and launches kingdomcultural communities and initiatives that destroy Evil and restore all things ruined by Evil. For more information, write Basileia, P.O. Box 60695, Colorado Springs, CO 80960, or visit www.basileians.com.

ISBN-10: 1534758917
ISBN-13: 978-1534758919

To all who journey with Christ in becoming
by Grace what God is by nature.

*But thanks be to God, who gives us the victory
through our Lord Jesus Christ.*

1 Corinthians 15:57

Contents

INTRODUCTION

I will put enmity between you and the woman, and between your offspring and her offspring; he shall crush your head, and you shall bruise his heel.

Genesis 3:15

The work of Christ is first and foremost a victory over the powers which hold mankind in bondage: sin, death, and the devil.

Irenaeus

*C*HRISTUS VICTOR, WHICH MEANS "CHRIST VICTORIOUS," is the view of the Faith embodied by the ancient Church, still held by the Eastern Church, and that many in the Western Church are rediscovering today. It is the view of the Faith held by Basileia.

In much of the Western Church today, Jesus might as well be called *Christus Victim* instead of *Christus Victor*. But this is changing. Thanks be to God.

In the *Christus Victim* view of salvation, Christ's death and resurrection is the end of His saving mission, which in the

9

end accomplishes the salvation of some people and some things, but not all. But in the *Christus Victor* view, Christ's death and resurrection is just the beginning of the age-to-age process of "the restoration of all things" (Acts 3:21).

Jesus is not a sacrificial *victim* sent to satisfy God's wrath so that we can merely be forgiven of the guilt of our sins and go to heaven when we die. This narrow, pathetic view of the Gospel is not the Gospel, but the Word of God forsaken by human tradition—a tradition of the fallen world not according to the truth revealed by our Father in heaven. God has something far greater in store for us than just wiping away the guilt of our sins, as great as that is. Jesus as Word made flesh is now *Victor* over the power of Evil itself, that is, over Death, sin, and Satan. Thus, salvation isn't merely a future hope of going from earth to heaven when we die, but the experience of God's Kingdom coming from heaven to earth *in and through us now* while we live.

The *Christus Victor* story sees Christ's death *and* resurrection within the broader context of the Incarnation, making salvation a greater story than I suspect most of us have yet dared to imagine. In the Incarnation, the image of God in Mankind corrupted in Adam's fall is restored in Christ. And since Mankind's corruption plunged creation into ruin, Mankind's restoration in Christ sets in motion the restoration of *all things* destroyed by Evil. Dare to imagine that.

Christ doesn't just save us from our sins; He saves *everything*.

Christus Victor saves everything in the heavens and on earth, including the heavens and the earth. The mistaken view that Evil has so ruined things that one day God will destroy the physical heavens and earth and start over is paganism, not the Faith once and for all delivered to the Saints. The pagan worldview believes that Evil inseparably and permanently fuses with certain people and things making them unredeemable, justifying their "destruction" by annihilation or by being permanently warehoused in "hell." This view of "destruction" is pagan to the core and has compromised much that is called "preaching the gospel" today. The idea that Evil can have a *permanent* effect or future in God's universe is not the Gospel of Jesus Christ. *Christus Victor* destroys Evil and restores everything ruined by Evil. That's the Gospel.

Christus Victor's destruction of Evil and restoration of all things ruined by Evil is the answer that many seek today to the problem of Evil.

The pagan worldview sees judgment in one-dimensional terms as the "destruction" of some or even all things ruined by Evil. The pagan worldview has no way of separating the things destroyed by Evil from Evil itself so that the Evil alone might be destroyed and all things ruined by Evil might be restored. The pagan view leaves some things and some people permanently bound by the power of Evil with no hope of restoration. In this view, Evil as a power either reigns forever or exacts everlasting, irreversible damage on people and creation. Then the traditions of fallen Mankind kick in and declare that all damaged goods must be thrown out with the trash. Paganized concepts of judgment have infiltrated much Christian thinking today, mainly in the West, reducing the Gospel to a spiritualized, sentimentalized, sanitized, lukewarm message about how a few of us can get out of life alive while the rest of humanity and creation burn or get snuffed out of existence. Such a pitiful, wretched "gospel" does not answer the problem of Evil but perpetuates it.

In sharp contrast to the *Christus Victim* view, the *Christus Victor* view proclaims a marvelous, mysterious, and multi-dimensional view of judgment that first separates Evil from what it has ruined so that Evil alone gets destroyed, and everything that Evil has ruined gets restored. The *Christus Victor* view is the strapping, self-authenticating, profoundly satisfying answer to the problem of Evil. What is God doing about Evil in people and creation? He's destroying it. That's what He's doing, but in a way that at the same time *restores* all people and everything in creation ruined by Evil.

Jesus knew His death and resurrection would unleash a unique, never before seen kind of judgment that would accomplish both the destruction of Evil and the restoration of all things ruined by Evil. He said, "Now is the judgment of this world; now the ruler of this world will be cast out. And I, if I am lifted up from the earth, will draw all to Myself" (Jn. 12:31-32). Christ's death is the death of Death, sin, and Satan. The kind of death that Christ exacts on Evil is permanent and irreversible. But the kind of mortality that Evil exacts on people and creation is *not* permanent and is reversible. Evil is not as powerful as good. Good overcomes Evil. Christ's resurrection makes the death and destruction that all people and creation experience temporary and reversible. While all people and all things in creation ruined in Adam do indeed die, in Christ they are all made alive again (1 Cor. 15:22). The only thing not coming back from the dead is Evil itself.

In *Christus Victor*, there are two distinct types of death and destruction. First, Evil's *power* of destruction is defeated and disarmed by Christ's death. Second, Evil's destructive effects on people and creation are reversed by Christ's resurrection. While everything ruined by Evil will die, because of Christ's resurrection *death is not the end of the story for people and creation.* The type of death and destruction that Christ unleashes against Evil is the end of the line for Evil. But the sort of death and destruction that all people and all creation experience with Christ in His death is the doorway into the New Heavens and the New Earth. Paganism preaches there's only one kind of death and destruction. The *Christus Victor* view proclaims that there are two kinds of death and destruction—one that is the end of Evil and the other that leads to life on the other side of the Valley of the Shadow of Death for all things ruined by Evil. And so with the Church in all times and in all places we confess, "We look for the resurrection of the dead, and the life of the world to come. Amen."

The mystery at the heart of the *Christus Victor* story is *how* Christ separates Evil from what it has ruined to destroy Evil and restore all that Evil has destroyed. So, if you dare, I invite you to open up your heart and mind and explore this mystery in the telling of the *Christus Victor* story below, adapted from the *Constitution of Basileia.*

THE CHRISTUS VICTOR STORY

B Y HIS WORD, GOD CREATED, SUSTAINS, AND RULES all things in the heavens and the earth.[1] He created Mankind in His image to have dominion over the earthly realm, to cultivate and keep it as the dwelling place of God with Mankind.[2] By His grace, God empowered Mankind to rule over the earth by revealing the meaning of all things in creation, by His Word, and through the Spirit.[3] God only required that Mankind keep the covenant and live by every word that proceeds from the mouth of God.[4]

Likewise, just as God granted authority to Mankind to rule the earthly realm, so He delegated to angelic principalities and powers authority to govern the heavenly realms.[5] But Satan led one-third of the angels in rebellion against God and sought to establish an independent kingdom in the heavenly realms.[6] Not stopping there, aspiring to expand his reach beyond the heavens to the earth, he determined to convince Adam to become "like God" and cast off God's sovereign authority over him and the earth. For if Adam did this, then

---

[1] Gen. 1:1; Jn. 1:1-3; Col. 1:17; Heb. 1:3; Rev. 4:11

[2] Gen. 1:26-28; 2:15; Ps. 8:6-8; Dan. 4:32; Rom. 13:1; Rev. 21:3

[3] Gen. 2:16-17; Ex. 25:40 (cf. Heb. 8:5); Jer. 23:18; Amos 3:7; Mk. 4:11-12; Jn. 16:13; 1 Jn. 2:20

[4] Gen. 2:15; 17:9; Deut. 4:6; 8:3 (cf. Matt. 4:4); Is. 62:6-7; Matt. 28:20

[5] Is. 24:21; Col. 1:16

[6] Is. 14:12-21; Ezek. 28:11-29 (cf. 1 Tim. 3:6); Eph. 6:12

14

Satan could justly accuse Adam and all Mankind before God of being unfit to serve as the Lord's ruler of the earth.[7]

So Satan came to the Garden. He first deceived Eve, then tempted Adam. But neither Adam nor Eve bore witness to the truth—the truth that Mankind's kingdom authority is grounded, not in himself, but in God and His Word.[8] So they sinned, but not just as individuals. In his collective capacity and representative authority, Adam was not only Eve's husband but also the covenantal head of humanity.[9] Thus, Adam plunged the human race and the earthly creation into ruin by putting the voice of human authority above God's.[10] Death entered the creation through Adam's foolish, lawless[11] attempt to determine the knowledge of good independently of God and His Word.[12]

But before Adam ate of the Tree of Life (whereby he would not die), God excommunicated him from the Garden. While Adam would now certainly die, not just spiritually, but also physically, he could also be born again. So the Lord drove Adam from His presence, stationing cherubim to guard the way back to the Tree of Life.[13] And just as God had warned, Adam's sin plunged Mankind[14] and the entire created order[15] into the darkness and dust of death. By failing to keep the

---

[7] Rom. 6:6; Rev. 12:10

[8] Gen. 3:1-6, 13; Jn. 19:11; 2 Cor. 11:3; 1 Tim. 2:14

[9] Gen. 1:27; Rom. 5:14

[10] Gen. 3:17

[11] Rom. 5:12-20

[12] Gen. 3:22; 1 Jn. 3:4

[13] Gen. 3:22-24; Ex. 26:31

[14] Rom. 5:12

[15] Rom. 8:21-22

dominion authority that was his by grace, Adam's sin opened the spiritual doorway to Satan and Death, permitting these enemies to unleash hellish destruction throughout the earthly realm.[16] By his sin, Adam, as the covenantal representative of the human race, delivered to Satan the authority of the kingdoms of the earth God initially gave to Mankind.[17] By his sin, Adam crowned Satan as the god of the fallen world.[18]

But when all appeared lost, God intervened and revealed His plan to defeat Death, sin, and Satan and thus restore Mankind and the creation.[19] The Lord announced that He would launch a great war between the covenant-breaking seed of Satan and the covenant-keeping Seed of the woman.[20]

Although ordained by God from before creation, this plan was so bold and unexpected that the rulers of the Fallen World System never comprehended it.[21] They failed to perceive that this Seed of the woman—who is the Church collectively and Christ individually—would not fight with carnal weapons, attempting to defeat Evil by wielding coercive power like the rulers of the fallen world.[22] Instead by remaining humbly obedient to the will of God, Christ *exhausted Evil,* crushing Satan's head under His feet. But this radical road to victory would come at a great cost, for His heel would be bruised, resulting in His death.[23] However, even Death could not keep its hold on Him. Rising from the

---

[16] Lk. 4:6; Rom. 5:12

[17] Lk. 4:6

[18] Eph. 2:2

[19] Gen. 3:15

[20] Rev. 12:17

[21] 1 Cor. 2:7-8; Rev. 13:8

[22] Rom. 5:14; 1 Cor. 15:21-22, 45, 47; 2 Cor. 10:4-5

[23] Gen. 3:15; Is. 53:4-6

dead, He turned the greatest apparent defeat in history into the greatest triumph of the ages—the victory of the Lamb who takes away the sin of the fallen world.[24] Through the Cross Christ was crowned in His resurrection, not just with one, but with two great victories.[25] With one blow He crushed Satan's head, casting him out of heaven,[26] *and* He destroyed the power of sin,[27] freeing Mankind and creation from the grasp of Satan and Death.[28] This one blow separated Evil from what it had ruined to *both* destroy Evil and restore all that Evil had ruined. Thus began the new heavens and the new earth.[29]

And so Christ, the last Adam,[30] by His obedience to God's every word,[31] was *given* the dominion authority that the first Adam lost.[32] He made the good confession that Adam failed to make,[33] confessing before Pontius Pilate that His Kingdom is not of the fallen world, rooted in the independent force and folly of autonomous human authority.[34] Instead, Christ, a king born to testify to the truth, confessed that the origin of His authority is from above.[35] He never did or said one thing by His own authority, but only in dependence upon His

---

[24] Jn. 1:29; Rev. 4:9-10

[25] Jn. 12:21-33; Col. 2:13-14; 1 Jn. 3:5, 8

[26] Rom. 16:20; Heb. 2:14; Rev. 12:7-9

[27] Rom. 8:3

[28] Is. 53:5; Rom. 6:6; 2 Tim. 1:10

[29] Jn. 19:30 (cf. Gen. 2:1; Is. 65:17-23); 2 Cor. 5:17

[30] Rom. 5:14; 1 Cor. 15:45

[31] Matt. 4:4; Heb. 10:7

[32] Ps. 8:6; 110:1; Dan. 7:13-14; Matt. 28:18; Phil. 2:9-11

[33] 1 Tim. 6:13

[34] Jn. 18:36

[35] Jn. 18:36-37; 19:11

Father's authority.[36] Thus, He lived the first human life as God had from the beginning intended Mankind to live. By His death, He forever sealed His perfect life and then by His resurrection permanently removed it from the clutches of Death, sin, and Satan. Christ now makes His life our own when we receive the bread that is His body and drink the wine that is His blood, doing this in remembrance of Him.[37] For it was not in His power as the eternal Son of God, but by His obedience as the Son of Man,[38] even to the point of death on the Cross,[39] that He definitively destroyed Death, sin, and Satan.[40] Through His obedience as Man, Christ utterly defeated Satan and redeemed Mankind,[41] permanently reopening the gateway into God's presence that had been closed by Adam's sin.[42]

Christ did all this for the sake of His Church,[43] the house of God, the gate of heaven,[44] the dwelling place of God with Mankind,[45] and the pillar and foundation of the truth.[46] Now He calls His Church as a holy nation to follow Him, voluntarily building upon the foundation of God and His Word,[47] exercising the kingdom authority originally given to Mankind, lost by the first Adam, but now regained by the

---

[36] Matt. 12:28; Jn. 5:17-30; 7:16-19; 12:49
[37] Jn. 6:53-58; 1 Cor. 11:23-26
[38] Matt. 4:4
[39] Phil. 2:8
[40] Rom. 5:15, 17; 6:6; 1 Cor. 15:21-22; Heb. 2:14-15; 17-18; 2 Tim. 1:10
[41] Jn. 12:31-32
[42] Matt. 27:51; Jn. 1:51; Rev. 21:25
[43] Eph. 1:22
[44] Gen. 28:17
[45] Eph. 2:22
[46] 1 Tim. 3:15
[47] Ps. 110:3; Matt. 7:24-27; 21:43; 1 Cor. 3:11; 1 Pet. 2:9-10

Second Adam.[48] Peter, by his confession, embraced this call.[49] Thus, Jesus called Peter a rock upon which He would build His Church. For Jesus recognized that Peter's confession, as the representative apostle of the apostles, was not based in human authority but upon the revelation of our Father in heaven.[50] By his confession, Peter chose to live like Jesus. In the years that followed, Peter declared that all believers who confess Christ upon the foundation laid by the apostles and the prophets are living stones.[51] By this testimony of Jesus Christ—in which believers acknowledge that God, not Mankind, is the final authority in all things—the Church keeps the authority given her to extend Christ's Kingdom throughout all creation.[52]

Christ, now ascended to heaven, is crowned with all glory, honor, and authority, sitting at the right hand of God the Father until the Father makes His enemies a footstool for His feet.[53] He has received the Kingdom and the dominion that Adam lost.[54] But Satan, although definitively defeated, is full of rage and seeks to make war against the seed of the woman, Christ's Church, against all who keep the commandments of God and hold fast to the testimony of Jesus Christ.[55] But instead of removing His Church from interacting with the Fallen World System,[56] Christ commissions His Church to go

---

[48] Matt. 21:43; 28:19-20; Acts 1:8; 1 Pet. 2:9
[49] Matt. 16:16; 1 Cor. 3:11
[50] Matt. 16:17-18
[51] Eph. 2:20-21; 1 Tim. 6:12; 1 Pet. 2:4-8; Rev. 21:14
[52] Rev. 12:11, 17
[53] Ps. 110:1-2; Heb. 10:12-13
[54] Dan. 7:13-14; Matt. 28:18; Phil. 2:9-11; Rev. 5:1-14; 12:10
[55] Rev. 12:17
[56] Jn. 17:15

into this fallen world, teaching all nations to observe everything that He has commanded.[57] It is by this means that He extends His two-fold victory of progressively crushing Satan's head and restoring all things.[58]

About Christ alone it is said, "Of the increase of His government and peace there shall be no end."[59] The Father's Kingdom shall come, and His will shall be done on earth as it is in heaven, "'not by might nor by power, but by My Spirit,' says the Lord of hosts."[60]

Before His final return, all nations shall pass through the Garden Gateway once closed to Adam but now reopened by Christ, to eat from the Tree of Life.[61] They will go up to the Mountain of the Lord and taught the ways of God.[62] No one will have to force them. They will volunteer freely.[63] In this way Christ is building His Church and the gates of Hades are not prevailing.[64] He continues to sit at the right hand of the Father in heaven until the Father makes His enemies a footstool for His feet.[65] Then the end of the present age shall come.

Today we rejoice that Christ bestows upon His people the Kingdom, just as His Father bequeaths the Kingdom to Him, that all peoples may eat and drink with Him at His table in

---

[57] Mat. 28:19-20
[58] Rom. 16:20; Acts 3:21
[59] Is. 9:7
[60] Zech. 4:6; Matt. 6:10
[61] Ezek. 47:12; Rev. 22:2
[62] Is. 2:2-4
[63] Ps. 110:3
[64] Mat. 16:18
[65] Ps. 110:1-2; Matt. 16:28; 26:64; 1Cor. 15-23-25

His Kingdom, exercising the ruling authority God originally gave to Mankind at the beginning of all things.[66] And so shall it be, from age to age, now and ever. Amen!

---

[66] Matt. 8:11; Lk. 22:30

DARE TO IMAGINE

Felson: Tell me, Behmen, are we going in there to defeat
             a demon or to save a girl?
Behmen: *Both!*
Felson: Ahh.

Season of the Witch (2011 film)

ESTROYING EVIL AND RESTORING ALL things ruined by Evil doesn't happen automatically. It requires heroes willing, like Jesus, to remain obedient to death.

In *Season of the Witch* (2011 film), the Teutonic Knights, Behmen and Felson have nearly completed their assignment to deliver for trial a girl accused of being a witch. But then the fuller nature of the Evil at work in and through this girl reveals itself—she is demon possessed. When exposed, the demon flees with the girl, holding her hostage. The truth is, all along she has been a hostage of Evil.

A hostage rescue is a supreme challenge for heroes in any age, whether they are Teutonic Knights or twenty-first century SWAT teams. While rescuers may have the firepower to take out the captors, they can't simply storm in with guns blazing, lest they inadvertently kill the hostages. Furthermore, rescuers can't pay ransom demands because captors who getaway today only return tomorrow with more hostages and higher demands. Hostage situations are tricky. The mission fails—hostages die and/or captors escape—if rescuers don't rescue the hostages and take out the captors *at the same time.*

In the opening scenes of *Season of the Witch*, unheroic priests indiscriminately purge "evil" from the land by hanging three women accused of being witches. Although it's doubtful all three were witches, to ensure "evil's" removal from their town, the priests hang all three.

Then the action shifts to a crusader battlefield where we first meet Behmen and Felson fighting "infidels." The story suddenly shifts when the commanding bishop orders the crusaders to kill "infidel" women and children. "A thousand lost souls for the fires of hell. A glorious day for the Church," blurts the bishop. "You call this glorious?," Behmen retorts, "Murdering women and children?" "Know your place, knight," the bishop fires back, "You pledged your life to the cause." "For God. Not for this," says Behmen. Felson and Behmen abandon the crusade, declaring they "serve the Church no more."

Destiny leads Felson and Behmen to embark on a truly chivalric quest—their charge to bring to trial this girl accused of being a witch, but who in reality is a demon's hostage. Faced with the dilemma of a hostage rescue, what will our Teutonic heroes do?

"Tell me, Behmen," Felson asks, "Are we going in there to defeat a demon or to save a girl?" "*Both!*" says Behmen.

"Ahh," Felson responds, realizing what this will cost. Chivalry destroys Evil (by taking out the captors) and restores what Evil has ruined (by rescuing the hostages). One ingenious blow accomplishes both aspects of the mission *at the same time*. By facing Evil's worst—Death, Felson and Behmen ultimately destroy the demon and save the girl. By their deaths, they cross the temporal threshold and join the pantheon of immortal heroes whose memory lives eternal.

Our heroes faced a hostage dilemma, "How do we destroy the demon and rescue the girl?" In the course of their journey, they discovered the secret. Likewise, God faced a hostage dilemma, "How do we destroy Evil and restore all things ruined by Evil?" In the Incarnation of the Son of God, we discover the secret.

"When I am lifted up," Jesus says, two things happen *at the same time*. First, Satan, the demon prince of the world, is cast out. Second, all are drawn to Him and restored (Jn. 12:31-32). With a single blow, Christ's death both destroys the captor and rescues the captives and then *sends them back home, to Paradise.*

The *Christus Victor* story is but the opening chapter of the story in which we learn not to fear Evil, but embark on a journey in which we return to dwell in the house of the Lord all the days of our life.

May the Grace of God be with you as you dare to imagine what it means for you "both" to destroy Evil and restore all things ruined by Evil.

In the name *Christus Victor!* Amen.

ABOUT THE AUTHOR

Boyd was ordained as a Presbyter (Priest) of the Church with Basileia on December 29, 2004 by Bishops William Paul Mikler and Wayne Boosahda and consecrated an Abbot Bishop on January 9, 2016. In ecclesiastical fellowship with

Communio Christiana, Basileia (which means "kingdom") is a future-oriented, Celtic-inspired, missional expression of the Church that imagines, cultivates and launches kingdomcultural communities and initiatives that destroy Evil and restore all things ruined by Evil.

Boyd is the founding Abbot of the Basileia Abbey of St. John in Colorado Springs, Colorado and also serves as the Presiding Abbot of the Basileia Alliance. Boyd and his wife, Sheila, happily reside in Colorado Springs. In 2014, Sheila and Boyd co-founded CenterPoint (www.centerpoint.partners).

The Icon of the Resurrection expresses Boyd's passion for Christ and vision for the Church. This image shows Jesus destroying Hades and building His Church. The gates of Hades do not prevail as Christ and His Church destroy Evil and restore all things ruined by Evil. Christ stands triumphantly upon a figure lying prone in the darkness—the personification of Death, conquered, bound, and defeated. He is building His Church by raising Adam from the dead. Christ defeats Death and the gates of Hades have not prevailed but are now shattered by His descent and have fallen in the form of a cross. Trampling down Death by His death, Jesus leaves Hades in utter chaos, littering it with broken locks and chains. Jesus pulls the first man, Adam, from the tomb by his wrist, not by his hand, because Adam cannot help pull himself out of this prison of death. Eve, to the left of Adam, holds her hands out in supplication, waiting for Jesus to raise her too. Various kings, prophets and righteous men who immediately recognize the Risen One look on from the right. Here is pictured the restoration of Adam and all humanity into communion with God. "To earth

hast Thou come down, O Master, to save Adam: and not finding him on earth, Thou hast descended into Hades, seeking him there" (Paschal Matins of the Orthodox Church). Christ's descent into Hades to bust up the place and raise the dead is an astonishing image of *Christus Victor* in his quest to destroy Evil and restore all things ruined by Evil.

Boyd looks forward to connecting with you at www.basileians.com and hearing from you at bmorris@basileians.com.

Made in United States
North Haven, CT
30 June 2023

38391232R00017